BASKETBALL STARS

BASKETBALL STARS

STORIES AND SKILLS FROM THE NBA'S AND WNBA'S BEST PLAYERS

CHRIS NAVALTA

ILLUSTRATED BY
ANDERSON CARMAN

Z Kids • New York

Z Kids
An imprint of Zeitgeist™
A division of Penguin Random House LLC
1745 Broadway, New York, NY 10019
zeitgeistpublishing.com
penguinrandomhouse.com

ISBN: 9798217151578
Ebook ISBN: 9798217151561

Printed in the United States of America

1st Printing

Illustrations by Anderson Carman
Book design by Aimee Fleck
Author photograph © by Shomari Smith
Edited by Angelica Martinez

The authorized representative in the EU for product safety and compliance
is Penguin Random House Ireland, Morrison Chambers, 32 Nassau
Street, Dublin D02 YH68, Ireland. https://eu-contact.penguin.ie

For Sandy—who's been on
my team since Day 1!

CONTENTS

INTRODUCTION
HEY, BASKETBALL FANS!

My name is Chris, and I am a basketball superfan. I started following basketball when I was 10 years old. I still remember watching the legendary Boston Celtics, led by Larry Bird, who seemed to make every three-pointer he tried. I might have stayed a longtime Celtics fan if I hadn't learned about my hometown team, the Golden State Warriors, in the San Francisco Bay Area. They also had an excellent three-point shooter named Chris Mullin. He immediately became my favorite player. It also helped that his first name was Chris.

Basketball is the only sport where the score constantly changes within seconds. Each shot—whether a slam dunk or a long-range three-pointer—can excite the crowd. To witness a player make one of these shots is thrilling!

As I got older, I worked as a journalist and wrote articles about a few NBA players. I got to know them on and off the basketball court. I learned that each player has a personal story about making it to the highest level—and it wasn't easy! The journey to playing professional basketball is full of obstacles and challenges.

In this book, you will read about 10 players who succeeded in their own way. Each of them also had personal issues and challenges they needed to overcome. At the end of every story, you'll learn about each player's unique skills. I'll explain all you need to know so you can work on your skills, too! This book won't turn you into the next basketball star, but it can be the first step in your basketball journey. At the very least, you'll know why so many people in the United States and worldwide have such fun playing and watching this sport.

Ready for tip-off? Let's go!

STEPHEN CURRY

BIRTH DATE
March 14, 1988

POSITION
Point Guard

HOMETOWN
Charlotte, North Carolina

TEAM
Golden State Warriors

TOP ACHIEVEMENTS
- ★ Four-Time NBA Champion
- ★ Two-Time NBA MVP
- ★ Olympic Gold Medalist
- ★ 11-Time NBA All-Star
- ★ All-Star Game MVP
- ★ All-Time Leader in Three-Pointers Made

SIGNATURE SKILL
Supreme Ball Handler

WARDELL STEPHEN CURRY II—KNOWN SIMPLY AS
Steph—has played his entire NBA career with the Golden State Warriors. He's the only player to win the NBA's Most Valuable Player award through a unanimous vote and the only player to make 400 three-pointers in one season. He also holds the record for most three-pointers made in one season in both the NBA and college and is currently the NBA's all-time leader in three-pointers. You can even add *acting* to his list of accomplishments. When Steph was a kid, he starred in a few Burger King commercials with his dad, former NBA player Dell Curry.

It's hard to believe, but there was a time when Steph was not considered a star player. He was a great shooter in high school, but even the best colleges in the country thought Steph was too small and not quick enough to defend other players. Even though Steph is the son of an NBA player and led his high school team to three conference titles, he didn't receive a single college basketball scholarship offer from any major Division I school.

Virginia Tech, which his parents attended and was Steph's top choice, didn't offer him a scholarship or a spot on the team. So Steph decided to attend Davidson College, a small school of just over 2,000 students near his hometown of Charlotte.

By his sophomore year, Steph and Davidson qualified for the NCAA tournament, where the top colleges compete for the national championship. Nobody expected such a small school to be successful in the tournament. The tournament is divided into four 16-seed brackets, and teams are ranked according to their seed. For example, the No. 1 seed is considered the best team in the bracket. Davidson, led by Steph, was the No. 10 seed out of the 16 schools in their region.

In the first round, Davidson beat No. 7 Gonzaga University, a school where basketball is the *only* sport they're known for. Steph scored 40 points in that game. Then they beat No. 2 Georgetown University, another school known for basketball. Steph scored 30 points, and Davidson came back from 17 points down to win. Steph scored 33 points when they beat No. 3 Wisconsin. The team eventually lost to No. 1 Kansas, but it was a remarkable run in the tournament. Now everyone knew Steph Curry's name.

Steph soon set his sights on the NBA. But once again, he was criticized for being too small despite his accomplishments. The Warriors drafted him in the first round (seventh overall) in the 2009 NBA Draft. One of his teammates—Monta Ellis, a fellow guard—told the media he didn't think he could play alongside Steph because the lineup would be too small.

The Warriors didn't win many games during Steph's first few seasons. Then came his injuries. Steph was battling ankle and foot problems by his third year with the Warriors. The team nearly traded him to the Milwaukee Bucks, but the Bucks rejected the trade because of Steph's history of ankle injuries. Instead, the Warriors traded Monta Ellis—the same player who said the team would be too small if he and Steph were on the court together. Ouch!

By his fourth season in the NBA, Steph became a different player. His injuries finally healed, and Steph committed himself to be the team's leader. He got help when players like guard Klay Thompson and forward Draymond Green were drafted, and center Andrew Bogut, from the Milwaukee trade, was also added to the team.

Soon Steph became an All-Star player. The Warriors made the playoffs in 2013 and 2014. In 2015, they beat LeBron James and the Cleveland Cavaliers, winning their first NBA championship in 40 years.

Since then, Steph has changed the entire way basketball is played. Three-pointers are now just as impressive to watch as slam dunks. Players of all positions and sizes now focus on becoming better long-distance shooters. Today, kids mimic Steph's moves on the playground, trying to make three-pointers from the middle of the court.

With all his incredible accomplishments, it's easy to think Steph was born to be one of the greatest players of all time. But he will be the first to tell you it was his countless hours practicing and a determination to prove critics wrong that has helped him become the player he is today.

HANDLING THE HANDLES

Learning the game of basketball starts with being a good ball handler. Becoming a *supreme* ball handler has allowed Steph to excel at the game. This skill lets him quickly release the ball when shooting, or set up his teammates when executing a play. Balance is the key to supreme ball-handling skills. It sets you up for an off-the-dribble jump shot, a quick pass to a wide-open teammate, or leaving the person guarding you in the dust as they try to keep up with your dribbling skills.

PHASE 1

Begin with an open stance and keep your knees bent. Bounce the ball close to your hip and dribble outside your feet. Be careful when dribbling close to your feet because it's more likely the ball will bounce off your foot and create a turnover.

PHASE 2

Bounce the ball high enough to be somewhere between the knee and hip. For one minute, dribble with one hand, then with the opposite hand for another minute.

PHASE 3

Next is the crossover dribble. Here is where you move the ball from one hand to the other, side to side. The ball should either be bouncing off the ground or be leaving your hand. The time the ball is in the air between bounces should be as short as possible so the defender can't steal the ball (you'll learn how to steal the ball in an upcoming chapter).

PHASE 4

To perform a crossover dribble between the legs, repeat the previous phase. Only this time, bounce the ball between your legs from one hand to another. There should be minimal shoulder turns when bouncing the ball between your legs, and your feet should stay on the ground.

BONUS

To do a crossover behind the back, perform Phase 3, only this time bounce the ball from one hand to the other behind you. The key is to bounce the ball below your hamstrings and not below your rear end. Do not reach for the ball; wait for the ball to come to your hand.

The best way to practice these dribbles is to combine them together, similar to Steph's pregame warmup routine. Do each step 10 times. Repetition is key. Once it feels more natural, you will better understand how to control the basketball and set the tone in the game when you have the ball.

CAITLIN CLARK

BIRTH DATE
January 22, 2002

POSITION
Point Guard

HOMETOWN
Des Moines, Iowa

TEAM
Indiana Fever

TOP ACHIEVEMENTS
* WNBA Rookie of the Year
* Two-Time Naismith College Player of the Year
* Three-Time Unanimous First-Team All-American
* Iowa Miss Basketball (High School)

SIGNATURE SKILL
Step-Back Jumper

BY THE TIME CAITLIN CLARK BECAME A SENIOR AT the University of Iowa, she had already established herself as one of the best basketball players in the country. Between her signature moves, such as step-back jumpers and logo 3 shots—baskets made from the team logo at the center of the court—Caitlin has given fans many reasons to pay attention every time she has the ball.

Tickets to a University of Iowa women's basketball game increased in price by more than 200 percent once Caitlin started attending school there. In her final two years at Iowa, Caitlin and her team sold out nearly every arena they played, including away games. This was known as the "Caitlin Clark effect."

Born and raised in Des Moines, Caitlin started playing basketball when she was five. Her dad couldn't find girls' leagues in her age group, so she played in boys' leagues. Caitlin also played other sports, like softball and soccer. But basketball was her first love.

In high school, Caitlin played varsity basketball for all four years. She once scored 60 points in a game and led the school three times to the Iowa state tournament. In 2020, she was named Iowa Miss Basketball, awarded to the state's best high school girls basketball player.

In college, Caitlin led her team to the NCAA tournament all four years, including back-to-back appearances in the national championship game. By the time she left Iowa, she was a two-time National Player of the Year and the NCAA's all-time highest scoring leader—male or female!

It was a no-brainer that Caitlin was the number 1 overall pick in the 2024 WNBA Draft. She was selected by the Indiana Fever, a team that won just 13 games the previous year and hadn't made the playoffs in the last seven years.

Caitlin's success also meant having a lot of expectations in the WNBA. She was hoping that success would continue once she turned pro. But that didn't happen, at least not at first.

In her first WNBA game, Caitlin scored 20 points but also committed 10 turnovers, a new record for a debut game. Her team also lost by 21 points. Yikes! Overall, Caitlin was unhappy with her performance.

"Obviously I'm disappointed. Nobody likes to lose, that's how it is," Caitlin told reporters after the game. "But I don't think you can beat yourself up too much about one game. I don't think that's going to help this team. No matter who it is on this team, no one can do that with how they played," she said. "Just learn from it and move on."

As Caitlin and her team moved on, they continued to lose. By game 20, Indiana only had eight wins. Then came the Olympic break. By this time, Caitlin had been playing basketball for nearly a year straight between college and pro. A break was certainly welcome.

WNBA games were not played for a month due to the 2024 Summer Olympics. While some of the league's players represented Team USA, most, including Caitlin, took the opportunity to return home and rest. She spent time with friends, went on vacation to Mexico, and attended a wedding. Caitlin promised herself not to touch a basketball for at least a week. She even kept her phone off for a while.

When the WNBA season resumed a month later, Caitlin returned to the team refreshed, rejuvenated, and refocused. She began averaging more points per game after the break. The team won nine games (including five in a row) and recorded their best results since 2016. They also returned to the WNBA playoffs as the No. 6 seed, where 12 teams make the playoffs.

In her first season as a pro, Caitlin won the Rookie of the Year Award and was named to the WNBA All-Star Game. She also set records in points and assists.

The future is bright for Caitlin Clark in the WNBA. As good as she is now, she will only get better if she stays committed to improving her game and taking the rest she needs to rejuvenate.

THE STEP-BACK

Nothing gets fans more excited than when Caitlin makes a step-back jumper. What's great about the step-back is that you can catch the defender off guard and attempt the shot from anywhere on the court that's within shooting distance. Being an elite step-back jump shooter requires excellent ball-handling skills (see the chapter about Steph Curry to learn about ball-handling). It also requires fancy footwork and quick reflexes to deceive the defense and create space for yourself.

PHASE 1

Drive to the basket with your strong hand. Keep your shoulders down to attack your defender. They will assume you are going for a layup and will continue following you.

PHASE 2

While you drive to the basket, use your front foot to push away from the defender and create space for your shot. Timing is important. It should be done in your initial drive to the basket—not too early and not too late. Step back diagonally at about 45 degrees.

PHASE 3

Whichever foot you use to push off, be sure to land with the other foot. This will allow you to stay balanced when your lead foot returns with your back foot.

PHASE 4

You should have time to attempt your shot if you've created enough space. For a quick jumper, keep your knees bent, and be sure to keep weight on your feet.

PHASE 5

Keep your shoulders forward as you try your shot. The ball should be well on its way to the basket by the time your defender recovers.

Like any skill you learn here, being an excellent step-back shooter takes practice and repetition. Try this shot alone and from different angles away from the basket. Then, when you are ready, try your new skill against a friend. See if they can defend your shot.

JEREMY LIN

BIRTH DATE
August 23, 1988

POSITION
Point Guard

HOMETOWN
Palo Alto, California (San Francisco Bay Area)

TEAMS
* Golden State Warriors
* New York Knicks
* Houston Rockets
* Los Angeles Lakers
* Charlotte Hornets
* Brooklyn Nets
* Atlanta Hawks
* Toronto Raptors
* New Taipei Kings (current team in Taiwan)

TOP ACHIEVEMENTS
* California State Champion (High School)
* Northern California Player of the Year (High School)
* All-Ivy League First Team
* NBA Champion (with Toronto Raptors)

SIGNATURE SKILL
The Floater

IT SEEMED LIKE ALL HIS LIFE, JEREMY LIN HAD TO confront his critics. When evaluating players before the NBA Draft, one coach wrote that Jeremy "does not seem confident at all." A few years before that, when Jeremy was a freshman at Harvard, one of his coaches considered him "the weakest guy on the team."

Jeremy's father introduced him and his two brothers to the game of basketball when they were growing up in Palo Alto, California, a Bay Area suburb just south of San Francisco. He would take the boys to the local YMCA to play pick-up games and show them old NBA games recorded on VHS tapes. The boys were hooked.

Many parents have high academic expectations for their children. Jeremy's mom was no different. She expected A's from her kids, but also supported whatever passions her sons wanted to pursue. Her friends did not understand why she let little Jeremy play so often.

"Growing up, some of my mom's friends would tell her that she was wasting everyone's time by letting me play so much basketball," Jeremy once said in a newspaper interview. "And so she would get criticized, but she let me play because she saw that basketball made me happy."

Soon, Jeremy began to stand out as a young player. In high school, he was named captain of the basketball team and led them to the state championship. He was also named Northern California Player of the Year.

Jeremy didn't get any basketball scholarships, so he

chose to attend Harvard University, where he continued to dominate on the basketball court. At Harvard, he was named to the All-Ivy League Team three times, including a unanimous pick for the All-Ivy League First Team.

When Jeremy decided to go pro, he wasn't drafted by any team, most likely because the scouting report said he wasn't confident. He eventually signed with his hometown team, the Golden State Warriors, but he didn't play much that first year and was ultimately let go by the end of the season. The Houston Rockets claimed Jeremy, but they released him just 12 days later. Jeremy didn't play a single game for Houston during that time.

Jeremy was then claimed by the New York Knicks, but it wasn't a warm welcome. At the team hotel, Jeremy approached one of his new teammates, Tyson Chandler, but Tyson thought he was a fan who snuck into the hotel. When Jeremy arrived at the arena for practice, security kept asking for his employment badge to show proof he belonged there.

When the season started, the Knicks won six out of their first 10 games. But then, the team started to lose—a lot! Over the next 13 games, New York won just two. As the Knicks prepared for their game against the New Jersey Nets, Jeremy got a call from his agent. He said that if he didn't play well, he might never play in the NBA again.

That night, Jeremy gave it everything he had. He wound up with 25 points, seven assists, and five rebounds.

The Knicks won. In the next game against the Utah Jazz, Jeremy started for the first time in his career. He had 28 points and eight assists. When they played the Washington Wizards, Jeremy scored 23 points and picked up 10 assists for his first double-double. That's when a player makes 10 or more of any two of the following statistics in one game: points, assists, rebounds, steals, or blocked shots.

Up next were the mighty Los Angeles Lakers, led by Kobe Bryant. It was Jeremy's first home game as a starter, and he dominated the entire time. He scored 38 points, and Kobe scored only 34. The national audience saw the Knicks beat the Lakers in New York.

Four days later, Jeremy made the game-winning three-pointer to beat the Toronto Raptors at the buzzer. The Knicks went on a seven-game winning streak, sparking a resurgence among the team. They also made the playoffs that year. Fans called the experience "Linsanity!"

A far cry from being the player considered "not confident" and "the weakest guy on the team."

FINISH WITH THE FLOATER

The floater, also known as the teardrop, is an attempted shot when the player is too far to make a layup but too close to shoot a regular jump shot. It is an especially valuable skill to have when playing against taller defenders. Two things make this play difficult to defend. First, the opponent may anticipate you driving to the basket for a layup, and second, the floater's shot arc is typically too high for a defender to block. It's easy to learn how to make this shot. You can practice by yourself or with another person (preferably a tall person).

PHASE 1

Start at the free-throw line, or anywhere you can give yourself some space to move toward the basket.

PHASE 2

Take a step forward and use that same foot to jump, all in one motion (most likely your left foot if you are right-handed).

PHASE 3

Jump toward the basket— make sure the ball leaves your hand as soon as possible after the jump.

PHASE 4

When releasing the ball, give it a high arc, like a rainbow (this makes the shot difficult for defenders to block).

If you play basketball against taller players, the floater is a good skill to have in your overall game. It will keep the defense on their toes and guessing the next time you try to attack the basket. Feel free to also have different starting points—not just the free-throw line. Overall the floater is a game changer that every small player should have in their bag of tricks.

GIANNIS ANTETOKOUNMPO

BIRTH DATE
December 6, 1994

POSITION
Power Forward

HOMETOWN
Athens, Greece

TEAM
Milwaukee Bucks

TOP ACHIEVEMENTS
- ★ 2024 NBA Cup Champion
- ★ 2024 NBA Cup MVP
- ★ 2021 NBA Champion
- ★ 2021 NBA Finals MVP
- ★ Two-Time NBA MVP
- ★ Nine-Time NBA All-Star
- ★ 2021 All-Star Game MVP

SIGNATURE SKILL
The Eurostep

THE LIFE OF GIANNIS "THE GREEK FREAK"

Antetokounmpo is the story of legends. He was born in Greece to Nigerian immigrants. Although his family had little money when he was growing up, he still found a way to become an NBA champion.

Life in Greece was a struggle for Giannis, his parents, and four brothers. The family constantly dealt with racism and faced frequent threats of deportation. Because Giannis's parents didn't have legal status to live in Greece, they couldn't find stable work. Giannis and his brothers helped support the family by selling small items, such as hats and watches, on the streets. Giannis said the boys tried to make enough money to help put food on the table at night.

"It was tough," Giannis said in a TV interview about those lean years. "We didn't have a lot of money, but we had a lot of happiness. When we were struggling back in the day, we were all together in one room. We were smiling."

But when Giannis was 13, his life took a significant turn. He was outside playing tag with his brothers when he caught the eye of a basketball coach. This person quickly noticed Giannis's long arms as he reached out to tag his brothers and was convinced they would be good basketball players. He offered their parents stable work in exchange for training their sons.

Four of the five Antetokounmpo boys began training and playing for a small basketball club, where Giannis began to stand out. He started playing for a semiprofessional team in Greece three years after being discovered. His older brother Thanasis was also selected and became Giannis's teammate. They were each making under $500 a month. Even though that was more than the brothers made selling watches on the street, they still struggled. The two brothers had to share the same pair of basketball sneakers during the game. Soon, though, the entire country knew about Giannis and his basketball skills, and professional leagues worldwide showed interest in signing him.

After he turned 18, Giannis made himself eligible for the NBA Draft. The Milwaukee Bucks selected him in the first round. Giannis was only two months shy of his 19th birthday, making him one of the youngest players to ever play in an NBA game.

Giannis continued to improve his game. In his second season, he doubled his scoring average, going from 6.8 points per game to 12.7 points per game. By his third season, Giannis averaged nearly 17 points per game. By his fourth season, Giannis won Most Improved Player and became an All-Star for the first time.

The Bucks were now going to the playoffs every year, knocking on the door to win their first championship since 1971. In 2021—Giannis's eighth season—the team finally kicked down the door. The Bucks defeated the Phoenix Suns in six games to win the NBA championship. Giannis was the Finals MVP.

Even with a successful career, Giannis says he doesn't feel pressure to win every year. For him, surviving on the streets so his family could afford to eat and stay in their home was pressure. Becoming a great basketball player so his parents would never have to work again was pressure. Now that Giannis has overcome all of these obstacles, he simply loves to play basketball and never takes anything for granted.

EXECUTING THE EUROSTEP

When it comes to basketball moves, mastering the Eurostep is vital to your overall basketball skill set. This is important for smaller players trying to drive around bigger defenders. The Eurostep is one of the more deceiving moves in basketball. It can really throw off the defender's timing if they anticipate blocking your shot.

PHASE 1

To start, dribble toward the basket. In a game situation, a defender will likely be standing between you and the basket, facing you.

PHASE 2

As the defender is right in front of you, hold the ball with both hands. Step in one direction and turn your shoulders.

PHASE 3

Using the opposite foot, still holding the ball with both hands, step in the other direction and away from the defender.

PHASE 4

After passing your defender, you are now cleared for takeoff. Using the same opposite foot, once you land, you also finish your move by making the layup.

The Eurostep can be practiced alone using objects such as a chair as the defender. When you feel comfortable, try it against a friend. See if they can anticipate your next move or if you've mastered the excellence of the Eurostep.

A'JA WILSON

BIRTH DATE
August 8, 1996

POSITION
Center

HOMETOWN
Columbia, South Carolina

TEAM
Las Vegas Aces

TOP ACHIEVEMENTS
- ★ Two-Time WNBA Champion
- ★ WNBA Finals MVP
- ★ Six-Time WNBA All-Star
- ★ Two-Time Olympic Gold Medalist
- ★ Reigning WNBA MVP (three career MVPs total)

SIGNATURE SKILLS
Rebounding

A'JA WILSON IS CONSIDERED ONE OF THE MOST dominant forces in the WNBA today. Her 26.9 points per game is impressive, and she is just as good at rebounding, averaging nearly 12 per game in the 2024 season. And she was the league's leading shot blocker, denying more than two shots per game.

A'ja most recently entered her eighth season in the WNBA, all with the Las Vegas Aces. She was the WNBA Finals MVP, led the league in blocked shots four times, and won two WNBA titles and the league's MVP award three times. She also has two gold medals as a US Women's Olympic basketball team member.

In college, A'ja was just as dominant. In 2017 at the University of South Carolina, she won a national championship, was named the NCAA tournament's Most Outstanding Player, and became a three-time First Team All-American. Not bad for someone who grew up not liking the sport!

A'ja's father was also a basketball player who played professionally in Europe for 10 years, but she showed little interest in the sport as a kid. In fact, when her father signed her up for a daylong basketball camp during her summer break, A'ja wasn't happy.

"I'll never go," she recalled saying to her father. "I'll never be like you."

A'ja did go to the camp but didn't stand out among the other kids. Eventually, she learned to love basketball on her terms and got much better at it.

The truth is, A'ja wanted to be good at something. She struggled in school. In middle school, A'ja couldn't keep up with the rest of her classmates. She wasn't learning at the same pace as her peers and was often told she was lazy and needed to try harder. The frustrating part was that she *was* trying harder. It just wasn't coming together.

A'ja's academic struggles continued in high school. Eventually, she went to see a teaching specialist and learned she had dyslexia. That's a learning disability where the person has difficulty reading.

Now it all made sense to A'ja. Before her diagnosis, she put a lot of energy into basketball to make up for what she couldn't do in the classroom. By identifying what was behind her struggles, she could get the help she needed to be a successful student.

In college at South Carolina, A'ja's coach, Dawn Staley, became her biggest supporter. Funny enough, she had met Dawn at the basketball camp her dad made her go to. Today, A'ja and Dawn are still close, with A'ja even describing her as her "second mom."

Even though there's no cure for dyslexia, A'ja received support to manage her learning differences better. Building up those skills also empowered her to become one of the greatest players in women's college basketball and arguably one of the greatest players in all of women's basketball. A'ja thinks anyone with a learning disability should know they are not alone and that help is available.

RULING THE REBOUND

It's great to score points, but rebounding is a crucial part of basketball too. When the Las Vegas Aces won back-to-back WNBA championships in 2022 and 2023, A'ja averaged 10.4 rebounds per game throughout the playoffs in 2022, then 11.8 rebounds per game in 2023. An offensive rebound helps create second-chance points, while a defensive rebound can help set up the offense. The following are some steps to keep in mind when attempting a rebound.

PHASE 1

In a game situation, when a shot is being attempted, don't run to the basket for the rebound. Instead, identify who your defender is, as they will be going for the rebound, too.

PHASE 2

After you identify your defender, put your body before them to keep them away from the basket. This is known as "boxing out." This tactic will increase your chances of getting the rebound if the ball bounces toward you.

PHASE 3

Once your opponent is boxed out, and the ball bounces off the rim, jump as high as you can to the ball before anyone else does. Ideally, stretch out your arms to grab the ball at its highest possible point. This makes it difficult for others to grab it from you.

A'ja Wilson   57

Practice this skill independently, then with a couple of friends. In a group, one person can act as the shooter and the other can act as your defender, who will also go for the rebound. If you can master this skill, you will undoubtedly have an advantage over others in becoming a well-rounded player.

KOBE BRYANT

BIRTH DATE
August 23, 1978

POSITION
Shooting Guard

HOMETOWN
Philadelphia, Pennsylvania

TEAM
Los Angeles Lakers

TOP ACHIEVEMENTS
* Five-Time NBA Champion
* 18-Time NBA All-Star
* Two-Time Olympic Gold Medalist
* Member of the NBA 75th Anniversary Team

SIGNATURE SKILL
Pump and Pivot

WHEN KOBE BRYANT WAS SIX YEARS OLD, HIS FAMILY moved to Italy. Kobe's father was Joe "Jellybean" Bryant, a basketball player who left the NBA to play for a new European team. For little Kobe, living in Italy was not easy at first. He didn't have friends and didn't understand the language. He spent a lot of time with his father, attending practice and basketball games. The team even gave young Kobe a job mopping sweat off the floor!

Kobe liked to play basketball. Being around so many players, he started to copy their moves. During game time-outs, Kobe would show off his skills to the Italian audience. Slowly, Kobe and his family began to adapt to the Italian culture. They learned to speak Italian and even made new friends. Kobe also kept up with the NBA as his grandfather sent him tapes of games featuring Magic Johnson, Michael Jordan, and Charles Barkley.

Seven years later, Joe retired from basketball, and the family moved back to their hometown of Philadelphia. This time, Kobe was 13, and he didn't want to move. He loved living in Italy.

Once again, Kobe struggled to fit in. For the last seven years, he had only spoken Italian, so talking to kids and teachers was difficult. Kobe also didn't understand current American culture. He was never invited to parties or social gatherings on weekends.

Kobe spent those days alone in the gym, playing basketball. It was the only place where he felt comfortable. In

Italy, he learned basketball was more about fundamentals than athleticism—although Kobe was pretty athletic. Back in Philadelphia, Kobe decided to focus on the fundamentals of the game.

By the time Kobe got to high school, he was the best player on the team. In 1996, his senior year, he led his school to its first state championship in 53 years. Kobe received hundreds of scholarship offers from colleges all over the country. But he played so well that he went directly to the NBA.

As good as Kobe was, he never stopped learning. He constantly asked questions to the older, more seasoned players, particularly Michael Jordan. Even after Kobe became the leader in the locker room, he would still ask Michael how to get the best out of his teammates. And after Kobe retired, Michael was still the person he turned to for guidance about life after basketball.

Though he passed away in 2020, Kobe played in the NBA for 20 years, all with the Los Angeles Lakers. He won five NBA championships in those two decades and was named the NBA Finals MVP twice. He was named to the NBA All-Star Game 18 times and earned the All-Star Game MVP Award four times. Today, the All-Star Game MVP award is named after him. He also won two Olympic gold medals as a US Men's Olympic basketball team member.

Beyond his amazing achievements in basketball, Kobe Bryant is also remembered for helping many people. He and his wife, Vanessa, started a charity to support kids in need. Their organization, which Vanessa still runs, gives scholarships, housing support, and educational resources to families facing tough times. Kobe wanted to make sure that all children had the chance to succeed, no matter their situation.

All in all, Kobe Bryant knew what it took to be an elite basketball player, and he never let anything get in the way of being the player he wanted to be. He saw every challenge as an opportunity, and even when he needed help, he was never afraid to ask for it.

THE POWERFUL PUMP AND PIVOT

The pump-and-pivot move is a practical skill for any basketball player because it keeps the defender off-balance while creating space for your shot. Other players like Michael Jordan, Dwyane Wade, Kawhi Leonard, and Paul Pierce have used the same move—but Kobe's pump and pivot was different. Because he was able to beat his opponents with different shots, Kobe's ability to pump-fake the defense and pivot away from them made him very difficult to guard.

PHASE 1

While dribbling the ball, drive to the basket.

PHASE 2

Once you get close to the basket, stop and keep your feet on the ground. Act like you're about to attempt a jump shot. This pump fake should force your defender to jump and go for the block. But you still have the ball.

PHASE 3

While the defender is in the air, use your inside foot to turn 360 degrees clockwise. This will allow you to turn away from the defender while they are in the air and see the basket with no one in front of you.

PHASE 4

Once you land on your opposite foot, use that same foot to jump off and attempt your shot immediately.

PHASE 5

You'll have different options for shooting the ball: a regular jump shot, a floater (see the chapter on Jeremy Lin and how to shoot a floater), or a bank shot, where you aim for the backboard so it can bounce into the basket.

You can practice this as close or as far from the basket as you want, as long as you are at a distance to make a shot. When first learning this move, use an object such as a chair or cone to pivot around. Once you are comfortable, give it a try against a friend. See if you can fool them with this deceiving basketball skill.

MUGGSY BOGUES

BIRTH DATE
January 9, 1965

POSITION
Point Guard

HOMETOWN
Baltimore, Maryland

TEAMS
* Washington Bullets (now the Wizards)
* Charlotte Hornets
* Golden State Warriors
* Toronto Raptors

TOP ACHIEVEMENTS
* Led his high school team to undefeated seasons his junior and senior years
* School record holder for most steals and for most assists all-time at Wake Forest University
* Gold Medalist, 1986 FIBA Basketball World Championship

SIGNATURE SKILL
Pickpocket Steals

TYRONE "MUGGSY" BOGUES DIDN'T HAVE IT EASY

as a kid. Growing up in the housing projects in Baltimore, Muggsy fell in love with basketball, but at only five feet, three inches tall, he didn't stand a chance on the court. The average height for an NBA player is just below six-foot-six! To this day, Muggsy is the shortest player ever to play in the NBA, and he played for 14 seasons.

Muggsy was always the shortest guy in the playground, and he was constantly teased about it. When it was time to pick teams, Muggsy was often left out. At home, he'd sometimes cry and tell his mom how cruel all the other kids were. But he loved the game so much it wouldn't stop him from playing.

Muggsy quickly realized he could use his height to his advantage—not by jumping higher or shooting more often. He knew his size and speed were his best weapons.

Muggsy became the best player on the blacktop. As a defender, he was so quick and short that he could steal the ball and quickly run in the opposite direction. According to one kid, he was "mugging" everybody. Around the same time, there was also a popular TV show where one of the shortest characters was named Muggsy.

Once the nickname "Muggsy" stuck, the player began to live life through a motto he called "Heart over height." Muggsy once said, "If your heart is in it, nothing else matters." At Dunbar High School in Baltimore, Muggsy led his team to a perfect 60-0 record between his junior and senior seasons. When he attended Wake Forest University, he set the school records for assists and steals all-time—two records he still holds to this day.

Next was the NBA. Players questioned whether he could play at this level because of his size. True to form, Muggsy proved them wrong. His best years were with the Charlotte Hornets. As the team's starting point guard, Muggsy was the clear leader who directed great players like Larry Johnson, Alonzo Mourning, and Dell Curry (the father of current NBA player Stephen Curry).

With the Hornets, he was always among the top 10 NBA leaders in assists. When he left the team, Muggsy was Charlotte's all-time leader in steals and assists. He even starred in the *Space Jam* feature film with Michael Jordan and Bugs Bunny.

Muggsy Bogues never let his height get in the way. He used it to pass and steal the ball. He even managed to block 39 shots in his NBA career. One of them was against seven-foot center Patrick Ewing, and there's a rumor that he even dunked a ball in a game!

PICKPOCKETING YOUR OPPONENT

Playing without the ball is just as important as having it in your hand. And when you're playing defense, it's important to know when and how to steal the ball from your opponent. Stealing the ball is an art. It takes agility, eye coordination, and—most important—timing. You can commit a foul if your timing is off by just a fraction of a second. Or worse—your opponent could whiz right by you and drive to the basket. These steps should help you become a better pickpocket.

PHASE 1

When defending the player with the ball, stay low and keep your arms out. If the ball handler is taller than you, they are at a disadvantage because they can't dribble as well as shorter players can. This is how Muggsy was able to use his height to his advantage.

PHASE 2

Keep your hands at the level of your opponent's hip. As you read in the chapter about Stephen Curry and ball-handling, the ball should be dribbled between the knee and hip area. Pay attention to the cadence of the player's dribbling and time your steal correctly.

PHASE 3

During the dribble, move toward the ball while it's on its way down. This allows your hand and ball to meet at the same spot so you can reach for the ball and steal it from your opponent. But don't touch his hand. That's a foul!

Every attempt at stealing the ball will not be successful, but playing defense in basketball means taking risks from time to time. Don't be afraid to make mistakes when practicing this with a friend.

LISA LESLIE

BIRTH DATE
July 7, 1972

POSITION
Center

HOMETOWN
Los Angeles, California

TEAM
Los Angeles Sparks

TOP ACHIEVEMENTS
- ★ Two-Time WNBA Champion
- ★ Four-Time Olympic Gold Medalist
- ★ Eight-Time WNBA All-Star
- ★ First Player to Dunk in a WNBA game

SIGNATURE SKILLS
Reverse Pivot and Step-Back

WOMEN'S BASKETBALL TODAY IS THRIVING THANKS
to what Lisa Leslie gave to the sport. As much as she left
her footprint in women's basketball, it wasn't a sport she
initially wanted to play.

Young Lisa grew up in Compton, California, in southern Los Angeles County. She was raised by her mother,
who worked as a mail carrier before starting a truck-
driving business. Whenever her mom was away for work,
Lisa and her baby sister lived with relatives.

By the time Lisa turned 12 years old, she was already
six feet tall. People often assumed she was playing basketball because of her height, but Lisa was interested only in
tetherball and double Dutch jump rope. It took a friend to
convince Lisa to try out for the middle school girls' basketball team.

"I only signed up for basketball because there was a
girl . . . who was really popular in middle school, and I
wanted to be popular," Lisa once said.

On the first day of practice, the team was split into two
groups—right-handed players and left-handed players. Lisa
was the only player on the team who was left-handed. On
day one, she was already being separated from the team.
Lisa didn't like the feeling of being by herself.

Instead of quitting the team, Lisa vowed to learn all of
her basketball skills using her right hand. That way, she
could practice with the rest of her teammates. Little did
Lisa know she was about to create something extremely

rare in basketball. While most players favor their dominant hand (right-handed or left-handed), Lisa taught herself to play equally well with both hands! Soon, Lisa became an excellent basketball player. The more she improved at basketball, the more she wanted to play.

"Once you fall in love with the game, it's something you just don't stop thinking about," she said.

Lisa trained with her cousin and uncle, who taught her to become a more physical player. In eighth grade, she joined a boys' team. The players refused to pass her the ball, but all that changed when she started stealing the passes and turning them into points for her team.

In high school, Lisa led her team to the state championship. At 16, she got to play in another country as part of the US Junior National Team. By her senior year, Lisa scored 101 points in the first half of a game, causing the opposing team to forfeit the game by halftime. That same year, she won another state title and became the nation's best high school basketball player.

Lisa attended the University of Southern California and led the women's basketball team to the NCAA tournament in all four years she played. In three of those four years, she was named an All-American, one of the highest honors in college basketball.

When Lisa graduated college in 1994, the WNBA didn't yet exist, so she decided to play basketball overseas for a few years. In 1996, Lisa made the US Women's Basketball team for the Summer Olympics in Atlanta. Team USA dominated the competition, and Lisa set an Olympic record with the most points scored in a women's basketball game, 35.

The WNBA was created a year later, and Lisa started playing for the Los Angeles Sparks. Lisa's court abilities put the Sparks on the map. She played all 12 WNBA seasons with the team and won two league championships. She was also the league's MVP three times and made the WNBA All-Star Game eight times.

In 2015, Lisa was inducted into the Basketball Hall of Fame. Pretty cool for someone who wanted to play basketball to make new friends.

THE REVERSE PIVOT STEP- BACK

As a post player, Lisa is comfortable playing underneath the basket, or inside the paint. Playing center, Lisa scored many points inside the paint by separating from the defense and creating her shot. This was done through her reverse pivot step-back move.

PHASE 1

Start on the right side for this move while facing away from the basket.

PHASE 2

Holding the ball with both hands, begin your pivot by turning with your right foot while keeping your left foot planted. Once the turn is made, you should now be facing the basket.

PHASE 3

Now that you're facing the basket, take one dribble toward the middle.

PHASE 4

After the one dribble, plant your right foot, then use your left foot to take a step back. This will allow you to get separation from your defender.

PHASE 5

Once you land on both feet, go for the jump shot. When attacking from the left side, repeat the previous phases, but use your left leg to turn, while keeping your right foot planted to pivot.

PHASE 6

Try this five times in a row from the right side, each time ending with a made shot. Once you make five shots in a row, then try from the left side. From the left side, you will turn with your left foot and pivot with your right.

This move can be practiced alone, but you can practice against a friend to test the move's effectiveness. Because Lisa taught herself to be ambidextrous, she could master this from both sides of the court. With practice, you can master this move from both sides as well.

LeBRON JAMES

BIRTH DATE
December 30, 1984

POSITION
Small Forward

HOMETOWN
Akron, Ohio

TEAMS
- Cleveland Cavaliers
- Miami Heat
- Los Angeles Lakers

TOP ACHIEVEMENTS
- Four-Time NBA Champion
- Four-Time NBA MVP
- 21-Time NBA All-Star
- All-Time Leader in Points Scored
- Three-Time Olympic Gold Medalist

SIGNATURE SKILL
Spin Move Toward the Basket

LeBRON JAMES IS USUALLY ONE OF THE FIRST
players that come to mind when people think about professional basketball. He has four NBA championships, four NBA Finals MVP awards, three Olympic gold medals, and 21 NBA All-Star Game appearances. Sure, it's easy to view him as a once-in-a-generation player with a true basketball gift, but LeBron's story is about perseverance and determination.

He was raised by a single mother who struggled to find steady work. They moved around a lot when he was little. Sometimes, if it was a one-bedroom apartment, LeBron would have to sleep on the couch. The constant moving caused him to miss half of his class days in school. At one point, LeBron had to live with foster parents when his mom didn't have enough money.

When LeBron was nine, he and his mom were about to be kicked out of a friend's home. As they stood outside the building, a youth football coach in the parking lot spotted young LeBron and asked him if he liked playing football.

He turned out to be a good football player. The first time LeBron touched the ball in a game, he scored an 80-yard touchdown. The coach saw so much potential in LeBron that he helped stabilize his life and his mother's. When LeBron and his mom kept moving to different places, the coach offered both of them a chance to live with him and his girlfriend. In exchange, LeBron would get to practice every day, and his mom would cook dinner twice a week and chip in for rent when she could.

Even though he doesn't like to talk too much about the tough times he experienced, LeBron knows what kids like him want (and need) to thrive.

"The most important thing that we can give [kids] is structure," LeBron said during a speech at the opening ceremony of I Promise School—a school he started in his hometown in Akron. "They have the dreams; they have the aspirations . . . they just want to know that someone cares."

With his coach's support, LeBron immediately stood out as a football player. That year, he scored 17 touchdowns. He was so dominant that parents of opposing teams demanded to see his birth certificate.

But when another football coach introduced him to basketball, everything changed for LeBron. He started to play Amateur Athletic Union (or AAU) basketball with four of his closest friends. They would beat the competition across the city, state, and country. Once a child who moved 10 times by his eighth birthday and missed between 80 and 100 days of school, LeBron finally had stability. He didn't have to move anymore, always had a home-cooked meal, and attended his classes more consistently.

LeBron and his friends promised each other they would attend high school together and continue their success on the basketball court. After he enrolled at

St. Vincent–St. Mary High School in Akron, the whole country began to learn about this kid named LeBron James. His high school games were on national TV, and his team won three state championships.

LeBron became the consensus number 1 overall NBA draft pick in 2003. The Cleveland Cavaliers selected him. Today, LeBron James is still in the NBA and is among the best basketball players ever. He has played for so long that his son is now his teammate.

LeBRON'S SPIN MOVE

Being one of the best basketball players in the world means having a lot of moves in his arsenal. But it's LeBron's footwork, strength, and the quick spin moves toward the basket that often leave his defenders in the dust. Here, we will provide some quick steps to perform this move and have a strong finish to the basket.

PHASE 1

When facing the basket (and a defender), make sure your shoulders are low and leaning forward. This will have the defender believing you are going to attack inside. But instead, you're going to make a spin move outside.

PHASE 2

As you start to dribble toward the basket, make it look like you're going to drive inside the key for a layup. If you are attacking from the right side, take the first step with your right foot. This should cause the defender to slide inside along with you, leaving the outside open for your spin move.

PHASE 3

In one motion, use your landing foot (in this case, the right foot) to spin/pivot away from your defender and swing your left foot in a counterclockwise motion. Be sure your landing foot is pointing toward the basket. This allows you to have an open look at the hoop.

PHASE 4

Once you're in position, you are cleared to finish with a layup or any shot you are comfortable making. Remember that the spin move should be executed near the basket so you can finish with a close shot.

When done right, the spin move can leave opposing players' heads spinning. If you already have several basketball moves in your bag, adding the spin move to your collection will keep opposing players guessing what you're going to do next.

MICHAEL JORDAN

BIRTH DATE
February 17, 1963

POSITION
Shooting Guard

HOMETOWN
Wilmington, North Carolina

TEAMS
- ★ Chicago Bulls
- ★ Washington Wizards

TOP ACHIEVEMENTS
- ★ Six-Time NBA Champion
- ★ Six-Time NBA Finals MVP
- ★ Five-Time NBA MVP
- ★ 10-Time NBA Scoring Champion
- ★ Two-Time Olympic Gold Medalist
- ★ NCAA Champion
- ★ Member of the NBA 50th Anniversary Team
- ★ Member of the NBA 75th Anniversary Team

SIGNATURE SKILL
Fadeaway Jumper

WHEN MICHAEL JORDAN WAS ON VACATION IN Italy a few years ago, he noticed that residents greeted him by making goat sounds. It was an odd way to get a former basketball player's attention. But the sounds had a purpose. To those fans, Michael Jordan *is* the GOAT—as in Greatest of All Time.

Whether it's a spectacular slam dunk, a buzzer-beating game-winning fadeaway shot, or simply the shoes that some players wear in a game, Michael's influence on basketball is unmatched. Even though he has not played in the NBA in over 20 years, Michael continues to be worshipped by fans of all ages.

Michael's achievements on the basketball court are legendary. He is a six-time NBA champion—having never lost the NBA Finals, winning the Finals Most Valuable Player Award all six times. He's a five-time league Most Valuable Player, a 10-time scoring champion, and a two-time Olympic gold medalist. He is among six NBA players who received the Presidential Medal of Freedom.

Michael may be considered the GOAT in basketball, but he didn't start that way. Michael tried out for the school's varsity basketball team during his sophomore year—and was cut!

"It was embarrassing not making the team," Michael said.

Michael was five-foot-ten and skinny at the time, even for a basketball player. The coach offered him a spot on the junior varsity team. Faced with that embarrassment, Michael had a choice to make. He could quit basketball and focus on other sports—he also played baseball and football—or take the spot on the school's junior varsity team. At his core, Michael was a competitor, even in high school. He accepted his role on the junior varsity team and played that season with the determination that would set the tone for the rest of his basketball career.

Michael became the star player on the junior varsity team and scored over 40 points in several games that year. That season sharpened his skills, and he would even practice in the school gym before class in the morning. Determined not to be cut again, Michael always found ways to stay motivated and improve, even when his body tired from all the practicing.

"Whenever I was working out and got tired and figured I ought to stop, I'd close my eyes and see that list in the locker room without my name on it," Michael would say. "That usually got me going again."

By junior year, he grew to six feet, three inches tall and made the varsity team. In his first game as a varsity player, Michael scored 35 points. From there, he never looked back. Michael averaged over 25 points per game in his junior and senior years.

Michael became a high school All-American. The University of North Carolina, one of college basketball's most well-respected programs, recruited him. At UNC, he won a national championship, became a two-time consensus All-American, and was the National College Player of the Year.

In 1984, the Chicago Bulls drafted Michael to the team. They were desperate to have a star player to turn the franchise around. By his third season, Michael began to win the hearts of fans nationwide. He won his first slam-dunk contest and helped the Bulls finally make the playoffs. The team lost to the Boston Celtics.

The next three seasons shaped Michael's career. In the 1988 NBA playoffs, the Bulls lost to the Detroit Pistons. The Pistons' strategy was not to let Michael beat them. This was known as the "Jordan Rules," which meant double-teaming and sometimes triple-teaming him to make it tough for Michael to score.

For three years in a row, the Bulls lost in the playoffs to the Pistons. Michael was frustrated and decided to make some changes to his game. A year later, he got to show off those skills when the Bulls met the Pistons in the playoffs for the fourth year in a row.

This time, Michael was bigger and stronger. His new approach to the game included midrange jumpers and even three-pointers. His teammate Scottie Pippen also helped score. The Jordan Rules didn't work anymore. The Bulls finally beat the Pistons in the playoffs and won the first of their three-straight NBA championships.

After a short retirement, Michael returned to help the Bulls with another three-straight NBA titles, starting in 1996. By the end of his career, Michael was ranked third in most points scored all time and is considered one of the most decorated NBA players ever.

Today, Michael remains involved in basketball. He is a part owner of the Charlotte Hornets and has several current players signed to his Jordan shoe brand.

To this day, whenever fans ask, "Who is basketball's GOAT?" the answer is almost always "Michael Jordan."

THE FUNDAMENTALS OF THE FADEAWAY

Michael Jordan did not invent the fadeaway shot but is the player most synonymous with the move. Other players like Kobe Bryant and Dirk Nowitzki have also mastered this crucial midrange jumper. However, Michael's ability to make baskets using the shot in clutch situations is iconic. The following are some quick steps on how to execute this legendary shot.

PHASE 1

Start with your back to the basket. In a game situation, you likely have a defender behind you in this scenario. Shooting the fadeaway will require you to turn over your shoulder and shoot the ball while jumping away from the basket.

PHASE 2

Turn with your left shoulder and pivot with your left foot to face the basket. As your right foot swings around, that foot will be used as your jumping-off point when it lands.

PHASE 3

Once your right foot lands, you should now be facing the basket.

PHASE 4

Using your right foot, jump away from the basket in one motion while attempting your shot. This will keep the defender off-balance and prevent them from blocking the shot.

PHASE 5

The fadeaway is an off-balance shot that goes against the fundamentals of a regular jump shot. It requires more power from your legs and more wrist strength. When you don't add power from your legs or more strength from your wrist, your shot could fall short, resulting in an airball or a block from the defender.

Remember that it takes time and practice to execute this shot successfully. Like most of the moves you've learned here, feel free to try this shot on your own. Then, when comfortable, practice this against a friend. Be sure to try this shot from different angles and distances. Eventually, you will feel more relaxed and normal with the fadeaway. And before you know it, you'll be like Mike and make buckets with ease.

CONCLUSION
GAME RECAP

As I mentioned at the beginning of this book, every basketball player has a story of how they made it to the highest level. Watching games on TV, it may seem like their road to the pros was simple: only talent and height matter. But that's just a tiny part of the journey.

The stories you just read are examples of what even the best players in the world had to deal with to make it to the top—from being rejected by top colleges like Stephen Curry to being teased for being too short like Muggsy Bogues to making rookie mistakes like Caitlin Clark. Each of these players learned how to persevere through difficult times. They all had that burning desire to achieve greatness.

While reading about each of these players, you've picked up many new basketball skills that can help you become a better player. Learning these skills means you're off to a good start. But don't stop here. Continue getting to know more about past and present players and their basketball moves.

Remember, the purpose of this book is so you can gain valuable basketball skills while appreciating the journey all these players have gone through to make it to this level. Hopefully, you will be inspired to walk your path and create your own basketball journey.

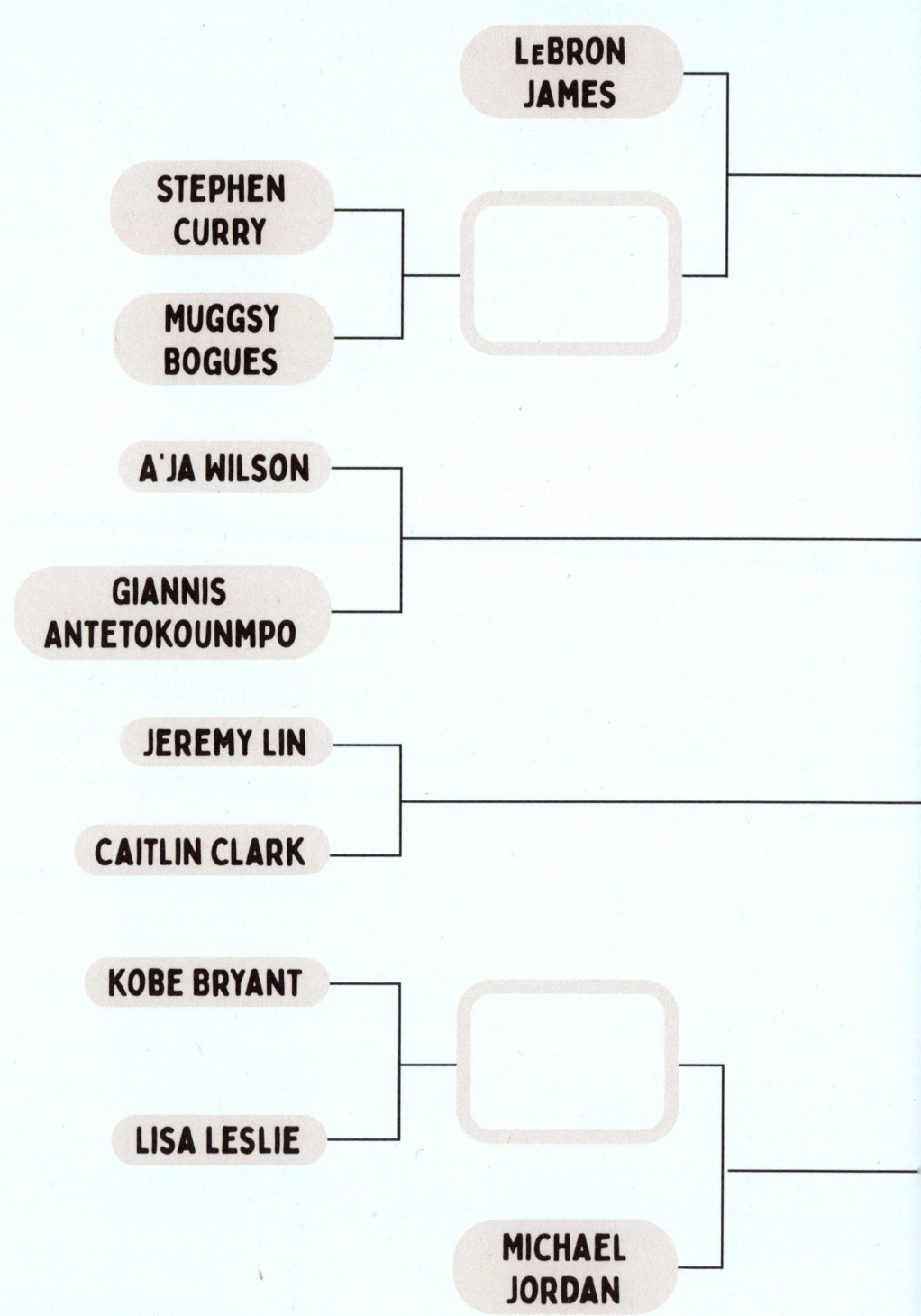

LeBRON JAMES

STEPHEN CURRY

MUGGSY BOGUES

A'JA WILSON

GIANNIS ANTETOKOUNMPO

JEREMY LIN

CAITLIN CLARK

KOBE BRYANT

LISA LESLIE

MICHAEL JORDAN

WHO'S YOUR FAVORITE PLAYER?

MY FAVORITE PLAYER IS ...

SKILLS I'VE TRIED

- [ ] Handling the Handles
- [ ] The Step-Back
- [ ] Finish with the Floater
- [ ] The Eurostep
- [ ] Ruling the Rebound
- [ ] The Powerful Pump and Pivot
- [ ] Pickpocketing Your Opponent
- [ ] The Reverse Pivot Step Back
- [ ] LeBron's Spin Move
- [ ] The Fadeaway

ACKNOWLEDGMENTS

Thank you to my wife, Sandy Navalta, for her ongoing support and for always reminding me "Who's the champ?" I love you with all my heart. Thank you to my family (Ludy Navalta, Pati Navalta, Julie Poblete, and Cicero Estrella) for your love and kindness. To my dad, Glorino Navalta: I miss you so much! Big thanks to the Zeitgeist team, especially Meg Ilasco and Angelica Martinez. It's been a great journey, and I appreciate the opportunity more than you know. To Gary Payton II, whose own personal story helped spark the beginning of this project: Thank you for your friendship and kindness. To Adonal Foyle, who I had the privilege to work with and ghostwrite some of his books: I finally have my own! And to Stephen Eriksen: It's been an unbelievable journey. I'll always be grateful to you.

ABOUT THE AUTHOR

Born and raised in the San Francisco Bay Area, **CHRIS NAVALTA** studied journalism at Sacramento State University. As a sports reporter, he began covering the NBA from 2000 to 2003, including several players in this book, like Michael Jordan, LeBron James, Kobe Bryant, and Muggsy Bogues. He joined the Sacramento Kings' Media Relations team in 2003. The same year, he started working as the publicist for Golden State Warriors player

Adonal Foyle, who he worked with for 20 years. Chris has also worked on projects with other basketball players, including Muggsy Bogues and Aaron Gordon. Chris loves basketball so much, he even got married at an NBA player's home. Today, Chris leads award-nominated PR campaigns in the gaming industry. He continues to work with basketball players, such as Gary Payton II, Karl-Anthony Towns, Jaren Jackson Jr., and Cameron Johnson, connecting them with the video games they love to play.

ABOUT THE ILLUSTRATOR

ANDERSON CARMAN graduated from Savannah College of Art and Design with a BFA in sequential art. He is the creator and artist of *Fear Hunters, Cyber League Baseball,* and *Stan, the Green Flamingo.* He previously illustrated *Soccer Stars* for the Z Kids Sports Stars series. He lives in Atlanta, Georgia, with his wife and three kids. He was a gold medalist in the Basketball Knockout Event at his 2024 Family Reunion Olympics.

LOVE READING ABOUT SPORTS STARS?

READ ALL ABOUT THEM IN OUR SPORTS STARS SERIES!

Dive into the inspiring journeys of your favorite players and discover how they rose to fame and the skills that set them apart.

SOCCER STARS
STORIES AND SKILLS FROM THE WORLD'S BEST PLAYERS
By Travis DiLeo

Engage with winning soccer strategies, signature skills, and captivating life stories about professional soccer's biggest legends.

BASKETBALL STARS
STORIES AND SKILLS FROM THE NBA'S AND WNBA'S BEST PLAYERS
By Chris Navalta

Explore the journeys of ten basketball stars on their rise to greatness and the incredible life lessons they learned along the way.

Parents and caregivers can learn more about these books and upcoming titles at **zeitgeistpublishing.com**.

Hi, parents and caregivers,

We hope your child enjoyed *Basketball Stars*. If you have any questions or concerns about this book, or have received a damaged copy, please contact customerservice@penguinrandomhouse.com. We're here and happy to help.

Also, please consider writing a review on your favorite retailer's website to let others know what you and your child thought of the book!

Sincerely,
The Zeitgeist Team